I is for Idea

An Inventions Alphabet

Written by Marcia Schonberg and Illustrated by Kandy Radzinski

Sleeping Bear Press™

310 North Main Street, Suite 300
Chelsea, MI 48118
www.sleepingbearpress.com

© 2005 Thomson Gale, a part of the Thomson Corporation.

Thomson, Star Logo and Sleeping Bear Press are trademarks
and Gale is a registered trademark used herein under license.

Printed and bound in Canada.

10 9 8 7 6 5 4 3 2 (case)
10 9 8 7 6 5 4 3 2 1 (pbk)

Library of Congress Cataloging-in-Publication Data

Schonberg, Marcia.
I is for idea : an inventions alphabet / by Marcia Schonberg;
illustrated by Kandy Radzinski.
p. cm.
Summary: "An A to Z introduction to modern inventions such as computers,
microwave, umbrella, zipper and many more. Each invention is introduced with
a poem and includes detailed-filled expository text"—Provided by publisher.

pbk ISBN-13: 978-1-58536-327-8   case ISBN-13: 978-1-58536-257-8
    ISBN-10: 1-58536-327-8   ISBN-10: 1-58536-257-3

1. Inventions—Juvenile literature. 2. English language—Alphabet—Juvenile
literature. I. Radzinski, Kandy. II. Title.
T48.S415 2005
600—dc22   2005006391

To the inventors, innovators, researchers, and clinicians whose contributions helped me become a cancer survivor—within the months between writing this manuscript and receiving my first copy of the finished book. To my editors at Sleeping Bear Press and devoted family, I thank you for your generosity and support. And to readers of all ages, I hope you will find inspiration to make the world better, one invention at a time.

MARCIA

*To my li'l brother, Mark Williams
and Lisa and Addie*

KANDY

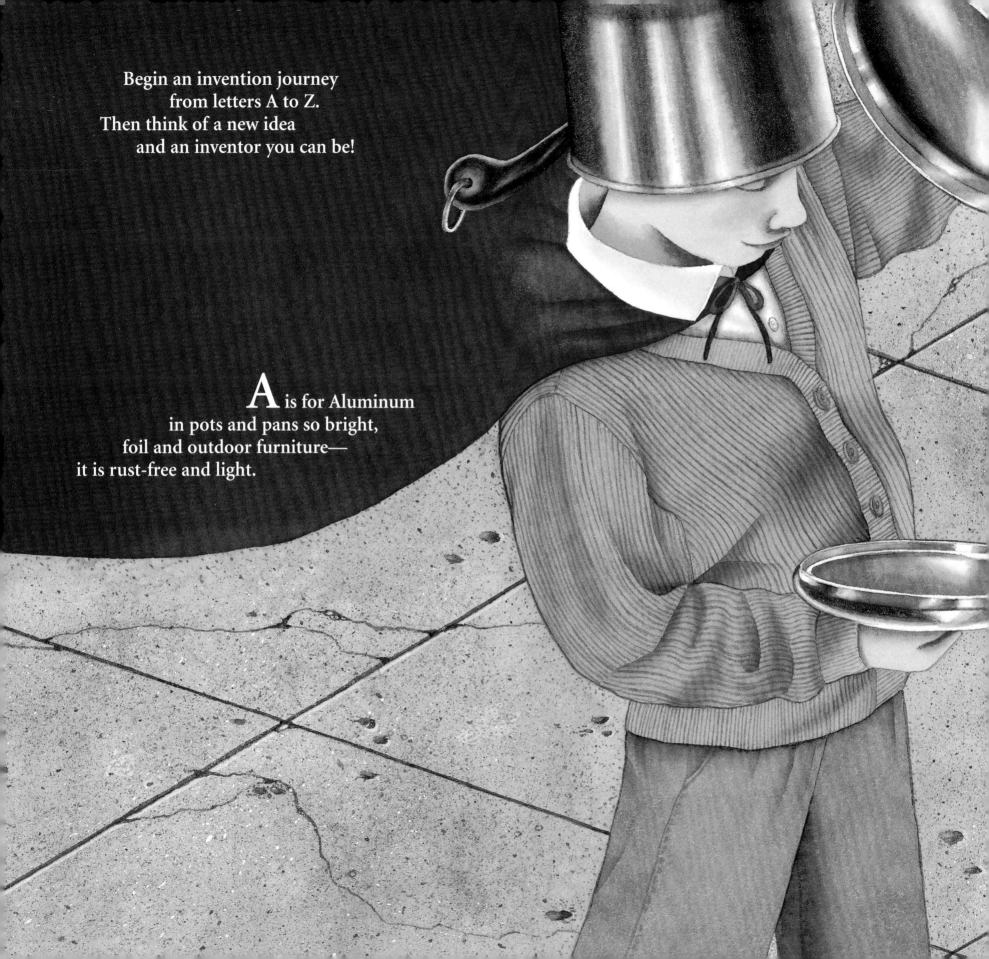

Begin an invention journey
from letters A to Z.
Then think of a new idea
and an inventor you can be!

A is for Aluminum
in pots and pans so bright,
foil and outdoor furniture—
it is rust-free and light.

Look around your home for items manufactured from aluminum. You might find food containers, beverage cans, and aluminum foil in the kitchen or patio furniture on the porch.

We take these inexpensive products for granted. Long ago—from ancient times until the late nineteenth century—aluminum was almost as precious as gold. It was plentiful, but difficult and expensive to remove from the earth.

Inventor Charles Martin Hall became interested in figuring out a way to refine aluminum when he was in high school. Later, his college chemistry professor encouraged him. Together they created equipment and prepared chemicals for Hall's experiments. Finally, after Hall graduated and set up a lab in the family woodshed, he invented the process for separating aluminum from aluminum oxide found in the Earth's crust. He received the patent for his invention in 1899.

During the same time, another chemist, Paul Heroult, experimented with aluminum in France and invented the same process. Through Hall's process and the company he started, which later became Alcoa, the price of aluminum became affordable. It is used throughout the world because it is lightweight, rust-free. and recyclable.

Pedaling your shiny **B**ike
puts a grin upon your face,
but riding an old boneshaker
would hardly win a race.

Boneshakers would not win a race today, but by 1868 bicycle racing became a popular pastime. The nickname "boneshakers" described the shaky, bumpy ride caused by hard bicycle wheels hitting uneven roads. The larger the front wheel, the faster the bicycle could go. Some wheels were so high that it took a six-foot or taller ladder to reach the seat.

Bicycle history dates to the early 1800s, when German and French inventors created two-wheelers without pedals or brakes. Riders used their feet to go and to stop. One inventor, John Boyd Dunlop, never pedaled a bike when he improved his son's tricycle. In 1887 he placed inflated rubber hoses around the tires and invented the pneumatic (air-filled) tire, similar to current ones.

Cyclists today enjoy an easier ride. Thousands of trails provide a smooth ride for those who cycle instead of driving cars, in competition, or for fun. When the East Coast Greenway is complete, it will connect 2,500 miles of trails from Maine to Florida.

Cities around the world promote bicycle riding. In Copenhagen, Denmark, so many people cycle that there are parking garages for bikes. In two cycling-friendly cities—Denver and Portland, Oregon—biking trails lead from one part of the city to another.

bB

The personal computer combines the inventions of many scientists. Some inventions, including the integrated circuit or the "chip" (please see letter **R**), are used in many electronic applications.

Here are a few, but certainly not all, inventions used to create the desktop and laptop computers found in schools, libraries, and in homes. They are all improvements over earlier models—ones that filled an entire room. Computers provide fast ways to communicate—yet are based on earlier inventions. For example, the telephone, invented in 1876 by Alexander Graham Bell, provides technology for computer modems and audio connections.

Known as the father of computers, Charles Babbage developed the idea for a calculating engine in 1834 in England. He did not complete his huge mathematical device, but his process won him this title.

Much later, the Intel 4004 chip, invented by Marcian (Ted) Hoff Jr. and Federico Faggin in 1971, became the first universal microprocessor. In 1972 the microprocessor flew into outer space aboard the *Pioneer 10* spacecraft. Stephen Wozniak and Steve Jobs introduced the Apple computer, the first single circuit PC, on April Fool's Day 1976. It had 8k of memory and a monochrome monitor. Soon, other companies such as Radio Shack, IBM, and Commodore developed similar working computers.

PC for personal Computer
takes us to letter C—
and then to distant places
far from you and me.

Do you know how the computer mouse got its name? Inventor Doug Engelbart, who patented his first mouse in 1963, says it looked like a mouse when the cord was switched from the front to the back to get it out of the user's way. Alan Shugart invented the floppy disk, used for storing and recording information, in 1971. And ink jet printers? They entered the scene in 1976 when Hewlett-Packard sold a model for $1,000. The flatbed scanner and music synthesizer, both invented by Raymond Kurzweil, expand the original use of the computer. They are peripherals (extra pieces of equipment that work with the computer). Please see the H page for more about Kurzweil.

QWERTY are the capital letters standing for the standardized keyboard and touch-typing we use today. Look at the upper left corner of your keyboard to find them. The letters on all keyboards are in the same order, thanks to Christopher Latham Sholes. Before his invention, each manu-facturer could put the letters in any arrangement!

Communication known as the Internet began in 1969, followed by e-mail in 1971. After two decades of improvements Tim Berners-Lee, an English scientist, changed the method and speed of accessing infor-mation when he invented the network known as the World Wide Web, WWW for short. He developed the necessary parts of the web to make sharing information throughout the world easy and quick.

Alfred Nobel invented dynamite in 1867. During his lifetime, he obtained more than 350 patents. As a youngster in Sweden where he was born and Russia where he lived with his family, Nobel's parents hired the best private science, math, literature, and language teachers. Nobel's father and other family members were engineers and manufactured explosives. Taking their lead, Nobel experimented to improve his family's products.

He invented dynamite and named it after the Greek word, *dynamis*, meaning *power*. After this invention, which was safer and more predictable than previous explosives, Alfred Nobel took out a loan to build his first factory. Business exploded, not in the literal sense, but his products helped in building roads, tunnels, and mines. As he continued to experiment and improve prior inventions, the industrial uses led to great wealth for Nobel. His invention led the world into the Industrial Era.

Nobel knew that his scientific experiments affected the world. He also knew that others, in literature, physics, chemistry, economics, physiology, and medicine changed mankind. He decided to leave his wealth to those who made the biggest contributions. He provided the financial source to honor some individuals each year by awarding the Nobel Peace Prize.

Dd

Dynamite begins with **D**,
exploding with a mighty blast.
It breaks up rocks to build long tunnels
so trains can get through mountains fast.

Before Elisha Otis invented the elevator brake, there was no way to prevent elevator hoists from falling when a cable broke. His invention greatly improved elevator safety by preventing falls. This improvement gave way to the development of elevators and eventually skyscrapers.

The public learned about Otis's new invention when he invited them to watch a demonstration. In 1854 he asked someone to cut the cable as he rode an elevator high above New York City. He proved the success of his invention when his brake stopped the elevator from a crashing fall.

After this public display, business rose for Otis—department stores installed elevators and soon, because of Otis, architects began designing high-rises and skyscrapers around the world.

The tallest buildings in the world demonstrate the success of the elevator everyday. Currently, the Sears Tower, in Chicago stands taller than any other U.S. structure. It is second to the Petronas Towers at 1,483 feet tall, built in Malaysia in 1997. When completed in 2008, New York's Freedom Tower will rise above both, becoming the tallest skyscraper in the world at 1,776 feet tall with 70 stories. It marks the site of the World Trade Center. Do you know why this height was selected?

E stands for Elevator.
It gives a safe ride.
When the doors open,
just step inside!

Clarence Birdseye (1886-1956) was not the first to freeze food. In fact, pre-historic peoples froze their leftovers thousands of years earlier. He combined previous knowledge and scientific theory for an invention we enjoy today.

After college, when Birdseye worked as a fur-trader near the Arctic Circle, he watched Eskimos fish. He observed that during extremely cold and windy days the fish froze almost immediately. Other times, when it was slightly less windy and cold, it took longer for the Eskimos' fish to freeze. More importantly, when he did a taste test between the two, Birdseye could tell which fish froze quickly. The "flash" frozen fish tasted better and the texture was like that of freshly caught fish.

Birdseye experimented with the Eskimo methods in his home kitchen in 1923. He used flat candy boxes for containers. It took him two years to perfect his freezing invention. Five patents about preserving food by freezing were on file in the U.S. Patent Office before Clarence Birdseye invented the unique "double plated" freezer that made him famous. His freezer, unlike any others, freezes food quickly. This process keeps the fresh taste and nutrients, which were often lost during processes requiring heat and chemicals.

F for Frozen peas and corn,
  pizza and cherry pie.
They all stay fresh for a long, long time—
  thanks to inventor Clarence Birdseye.

After inventing the product of quick frozen food, Birdseye continued by designing freezer cases for grocery stores and even the insulated railroad cars needed to transport his food all over the country.

At age 26, Clarence Birdseye's patent number 1,773,079 and the freezing process he invented changed the way people ate and preserved food the world over.

Ff

G is for Gas masks—
lifesaving gear
that firefighters wear
when smoke is near.

Inventor Garrett Morgan invented the gas mask in 1914. He called it a "Breathing Device" and "Safety Hood" to help fire-fighters, chemists, and anyone who worked near harmful fumes and gases. Users placed the mask over their heads, breathed clean air from one tube and then exhaled through another tube. He hoped to assist firefighters going into burning buildings.

During an emergency in Cleveland, Ohio, he personally tested his invention. It became famous afterward. Wearing the mask, Garrett Morgan saved 35 workers trapped underground. The workers were building a tunnel when it exploded, blocking the workers' entrance.

News of how Morgan's invention helped rescue the workers was good for his busi-ness. Soon fire departments everywhere wanted to purchase gas masks. When some people found out that Morgan was an African-American inventor and son of a former slave, they did not buy his inven-tion, but the United States government did not hesitate. The masks protected the military in World War I and later.

Braille is a code made up of raised dots. Each set of dots, called a "cell," stands for a letter, word, or punctuation. Blind people rub their fingers across the raised cells, rapidly "reading" using only their fingertips. The inventor of this unique code, Louis Braille (1809-1852), became blind at age three after an accident in his father's harness shop.

The toddler loved watching his father carve and cut leather. One day, when his father was not there, Louis went into the workshop attached to the family home in a small village near Paris. He picked up one of his father's tools, and tried cutting leather as he had seen his father do. The sharp tool slipped and gouged his eye. It became infected (antibiotics had not been invented yet) and the infection spread to the other eye, leaving Louis Braille blind in both eyes.

Braille's parents sought special educational opportunities for him. In Paris, he attended a school for the blind. He learned school subjects and tried "night writing," a code invented by Captain Charles Barbier so his French soldiers could communicate orders without talking. It was a slow method and Braille longed for a way to read and write as quickly as those who could see. He used Barbier's idea of raised dots to develop his own system, which he finished when he was 15 years old. Another Frenchman, Pierre Foucault created a Braille keyboard, one of the earliest typewriters. It printed the dots and embossed them on the paper at the same time.

H can be for Hands
and the help they give each day.
They even act like eyes
by feeling what words and letters say.

By 1834 and a few improvements later, Braille's code reached its current form. No one improved upon Braille's system like Raymond Kurzweil. In 1976 he invented a print-to-speech reading machine. The Kurzweil Reading Machine (KRM) changes different sizes and fonts of text into digitized sounds. This affordable and portable device gives people with visual impairments the ability to "read" everyday, ordinary printed words such as homework assignments that are not translated into Braille. Kurzweil is working on a handheld version of his reading machine that will be the size of an electronic calculator.

People all over the world read and write using these inventions.

There are Inventions in our book
standing for letter I.
You can be an inventor, too,
but only if you try.

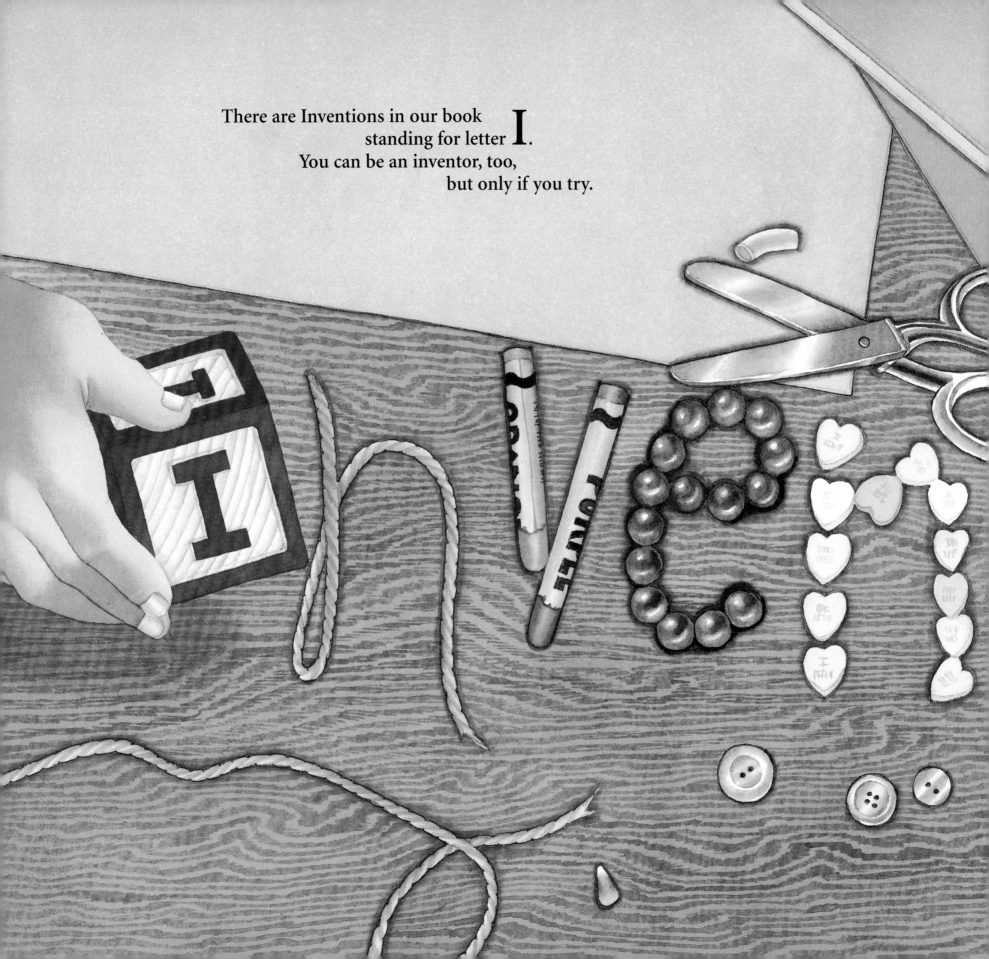

By now you know that new inventions are often based on previous ones. Inventors may patent one invention only to continue experimenting until they invent an improvement and then seek a patent for the improvement. It can take years of testing and refinement before the invention is ready for consumers.

"Necessity is the mother of invention" is a popular expression. Do you know what it means? Think of these examples for help in finding the answer. Elijah McCoy invented the lubricating oil cup so trains did not have to stop to keep parts in good working condition. He invented an ironing board after his wife said she needed a better way to iron. He invented a sprinkler because he wanted an easier way to water the lawn.

Inventions developed from the desire to make the world a better place line the halls of the National Inventors Hall of Fame, in Akron, Ohio. This museum displays many of the world's important inventions. Inventors are nominated, selected, and inducted into the hall of fame annually.

Ii

In 1976, passengers flew at supersonic speeds on the *Concorde*. The world's fastest passenger jet plane traveled between London and Paris to New York's JFK airport. It flew 1,350 miles per hour, making the trip from London to New York in just 3 hours, 20 minutes, nearly one-half the time of other jets. Fares of $12,000 were expensive and the *Concorde* stopped flying in 2003.

One hundred years earlier, on December 17, Orville and Wilbur Wright flew their historic *1903 Flyer* about 34 miles per hour during their longest flight of the day: 832 feet. The brothers took turns flying, but Wilbur piloted their aircraft for less than a minute at Kitty Hawk, North Carolina to reach this speed. The Wright Brothers studied the contributions of those who came before them, such as Octave Chanute who built a biplane and wrote about flying in the late 1800s. They built a wind tunnel to research their equipment—an idea still in use today as scientists design parts for air and space travel. They passed their enthusiasm and desire to fly faster and higher to each future generation.

Sir Frank Whittle and Hans Van Ohain coinvented the first turbojet engines. Their work contributed to the safe, high-speed trips of the *Boeing 707* in 1958. The *Concorde* and other modern day aircraft, including those used in outer space exploration, continue the timeline begun long ago by the Wright Brothers and aviators with the desire to reach new heights and speeds.

J stands for Jets
     crisscrossing the sky.
We've come a long way
          since the Wright Brothers' first try.

Kevlar® with a capital **K** has a symbol that looks like this: ® or this: ™. These symbols show that the word or design is registered with the United States Patent and Trademark Office.

Kevlar® describes the super strong polymer fiber patented by Stephanie Louise Kwolek in 1966. As a research scientist for duPont, a major research company, she obtained 16 patents, but Kevlar® is her most famous. After experimenting for 10 years, Kwolek and other scientists used Kevlar® for bulletproof vests. By inventing Kevlar®, Kwolek saves thousands of lives.

This substance is spun into a fiber with two unique qualities. It is extremely strong yet lightweight. Kevlar® is five times stronger than the same weight amount of steel. It works in water and high temperatures. Some of its uses include underwater cables, athletic equipment, aircraft and spacecraft parts. Tires reinforced with Kevlar® weigh less than those made with steel to improve gas mileage.

In 1996 President Clinton presented Kwolek with the country's highest honor for research and technological achievement: the National Medal of Science. She was inducted into the National Inventors Hall of Fame in 1995.

Used in bicycle tires and bulletproof vests in hockey sticks and soccer cleats—
Kevlar,® with a capital K
conquers the most amazing feats.

L stands for Lubricating oil.
Can you figure out how it came to be
that Elijah McCoy's invention
changed locomotive history?

Have you ever heard the expression "the real McCoy?" It means "genuine" and of high quality, not an imitation or a look-alike. This popular phrase resulted when Elijah McCoy invented a lubricating cup first used by the railways. People refused to buy an imitation of his invention, so they checked by asking "Is this the real McCoy?"

In the mid-1800s, as railroad transportation became popular, Elijah McCoy found work as an engineer and oilman. To keep the trains running smoothly, he spritzed the wheels and other moving parts with lubricating oil every few miles. The train halted so McCoy could jump off and do his job.

Elijah McCoy, the son of Kentucky slaves who fled to Canada along the Underground Railroad, was too well educated for his job as a railroad engineer. He was a mechanical engineer with an inventive mind, but he could not get a job in his field because of racial prejudice. While working for the railroad he solved the problem of stopping every few miles. He invented a cup that automatically dripped the lubricating oil when necessary—without stopping. His lubricating devices became useful on other machinery, too.

Ll

The Microwave begins with **M**mmmm
when it melts gooey chocolaty s'mores,
pops corn and makes applesauce—
speeding up our cooking chores.

Today, most homes have a microwave oven. In fact, the rate is higher than two out of three. We can hardly get along without a microwave to cook everything from snacks to whole meals. It cooks food quicker than regular ovens because it is more energy efficient.

Percy Spencer invented the technology behind this everyday appliance. He worked for Raytheon Manufacturing Company experimenting with radar used in the military. While standing close to the working magnetron tube he was studying, he noticed the candy bar in his pocket began melting. He did not feel any heat.

Because of his melted snack, Spencer began thinking about other uses for the magnetron tube. Production of the first microwave oven, called a "radar range," began a decade later, in 1955.

Most of us think of neon lights for advertising pizza, movies, and other businesses. You might not know that there are neon lights in your home and school, too. The little lights that illuminate off and on switches on appliances, and those on and around our computers are neon lights.

Frenchman Georges Claude invented neon lights in 1910. He placed neon gas in a thin tube and charged it with electricity to give off the popular glow-in-the-dark red neon color. Since then, plastic replaced glass tubes and many different gases create all the colors we see in advertising signs.

N
n

Bright Neon flashing lights
bring us to letter N.
The jumping colors dance and glow
through special rods that bend.

Cream Palace

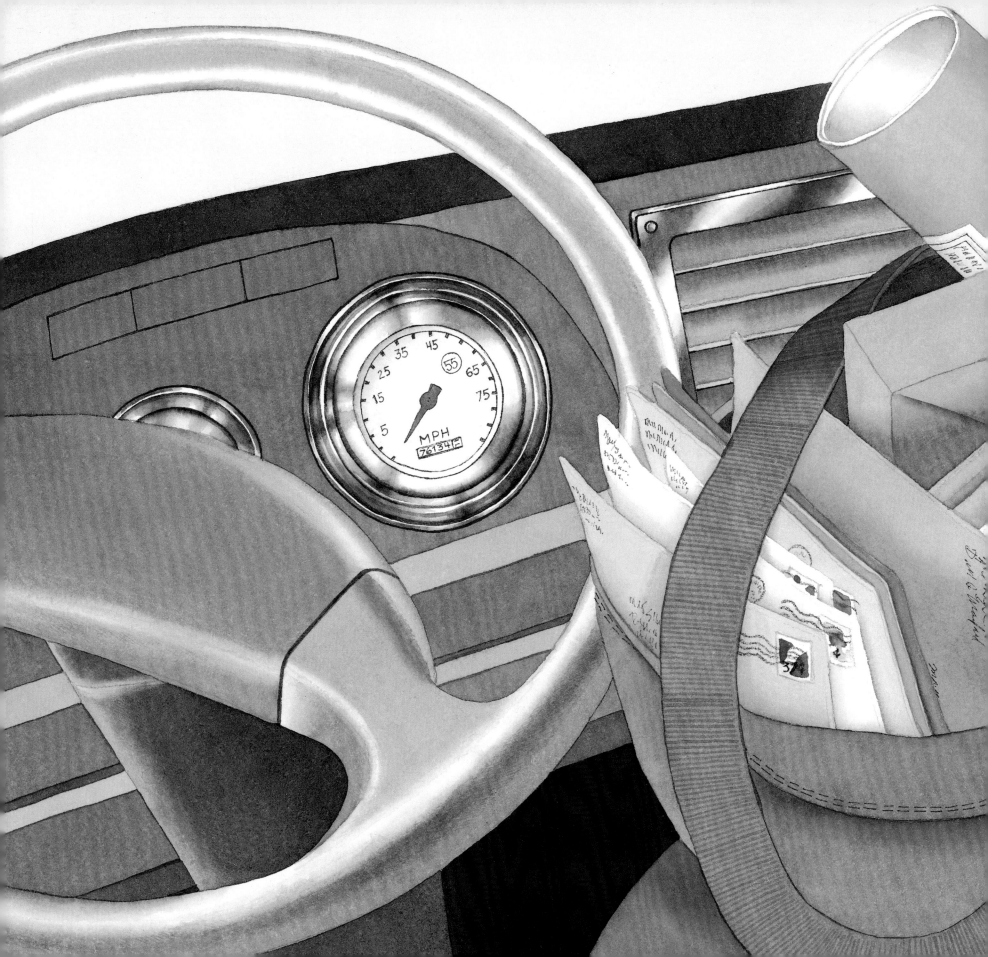

A more modern odometer was among Benjamin Franklin's many inventions. While serving as Postmaster General in 1775, he thought knowing the shortest routes for the postal deliveries would be helpful. He attached a simple odometer to his carriage and set out to plan the routes for workers. Later, odometers were used to measure the number of miles pioneers traveled each day on their way to settle the western frontier. Inventors of the wagon wheel device called the invention a "roadometer."

Can you think of any other useful "meters?"

Ben Franklin's invention—
the Odometer for letter O
measured the miles driven
by his postal workers on the go.

Pp

Peanut butter is just one of George Washington Carver's 300 to 400 inventions stemming from the peanut. Perhaps his most famous accomplishment leading to the abundance of peanut and other nuts was convincing farmers to rotate their crops. He taught them to keep the soil rich in nutrients by varying their field crops each season. Then he set out to find uses for the huge quantities of peanuts being grown. Oil, ink, and soap are a few of the hundreds of uses he invented.

Along with its many uses, the peanut has many names. Here are a few: lugume, groundnut, and goober. Do you know any other names for peanuts? One U.S. president grew up on a peanut farm. Do you know his name?

George Washington Carver invented the way to make yummy Peanut butter that we enjoy today.

Luther Burbank was both a horticulturist, a person who grows plants and trees, and a botanist, a scientist who studies plants. He created about 800 different fruits and vegetables. He helped feed the world by producing varieties that were strong and hardy.

He grew 11 different types of quince, a mango-shaped fruit that grows on a tree. They were more popular during Burbank's time than they are today, but they still grow well in California and are popular in Spain for making jams and pies.

Burbank's most famous invention, a disease-resistant potato called the Idaho potato, can easily be found in your grocery store, but in the mid-1800s he sent these potatoes to Ireland. He helped farmers recover from the Potato Famine when the blight destroyed their main crop and left people starving.

Patent laws did not apply to Luther Burbank's new plant breeds. After his death, legislators passed the Plant Patent Law of 1930 to protect his inventions and those of others who continued his work. This new law led to the growth of agricultural experimentation. In this way, Luther Burbank's contributions continue today.

Luther Burbank grew a Quince
with a taste of apple and pear.
Children in Spain love the tart flavor,
but in America, the quince is quite rare.

The invention of the radio occurred in the midst of many communication inventions. It is a good example of how one invention leads to another and another.

The telephone and the telegraph were in use when Italian physicist Guglielmo Marconi figured out a way to send wireless signals in 1895. He is credited with inventing the radio, but Nikola Tesla experimented with radio waves earlier than Marconi. Marconi received the Nobel Prize for his patents. In 1943, after Tesla held more than 100 patents and had 700 inventions, the United States Supreme Court reversed Marconi's patent rights for the invention of the wireless communication and gave the patent to Tesla. Tesla never knew these results. He died nine months before the decision.

Thomas Edison's lightbulb also played a role in the development of communication. Lee De Forest used technology from that invention to create an "audion amplifier." It was a vacuum tube invention making AM radio possible in 1906.

Many years later, three more scientists invented an even better way to broadcast sounds into homes around world. They were John Bardeen, Walter Brattain, and William Schockley. What was their invention? A transistor—easier to manufacture and smaller than vacuum tubes and they could be joined together to create more complex systems. As you might imagine, inventors soon sought faster, smaller methods.

Jack Kilby and Robert Noyce came to the rescue when they invented an integrated circuit connecting everything on one small board. Jack Kilby won the Nobel Prize for the integrated circuit in 2000.

To demonstrate the letter R,
turn on your Radio.
From this early invention,
came TV and stereo.

What about television? After Philo Farnsworth built an electric washing machine for his mother when he was 12 years old, he began thinking about televisions. By 21 years of age, he transmitted a dollar sign image and filed for the patent for his television invention. This patent began the era of electronic TV but Farnsworth continued—creating more than 150 additional television-related inventions.

Can you think of television inventions that you enjoy? How about the remote control? It was invented by Robert Adler, a scientist with Zenith Electronics Corporation. Orginally, the remote was called "Lazy Bones" and had a long cord. And color T.V.? In 1956, *Dragnet*, a detective show, was the first broadcast filmed in color. Later, the World Series and cartoons colored the screen.

The plasma flat screen invented by David Bitzer, H. Gene Slottow, and Robert Willson currently brings high-definition TV as one of the latest television-related inventions.

You have just followed along through a century of electronics. By now you might be asking, "What's next? A computer?" Check the **C** page to read about its history!

R r

Before sewing machines, hand stitching was the long and tedious method of sewing. Metal needles, the kind we use today, replaced the earliest needles—made from animal bones or horns. From 1755 to the mid-1800s various inventors tried ideas but none replaced the seamstress and the tailor.

Then an American, Elias Howe, developed a sewing machine using two threads. One in the needle on top of the cloth caught the loop of the second thread underneath the material and formed a "lockstitich." His invention worked! The lockstitch technique worked so well, in fact, that although he patented it, others copied his invention. His patent protected his idea. He sued others, including inventor Isaac Singer, for patent infringement. The court said he would receive money for every machine made by anyone who used his patented lockstitch method.

Isaac Singer's sewing machines, even though they used Howe's stitch, operated a different way. By mass-producing his sewing machines, Singer became a leader in this new manufacturing industry, and helped Elias Howe become rich.

Ss

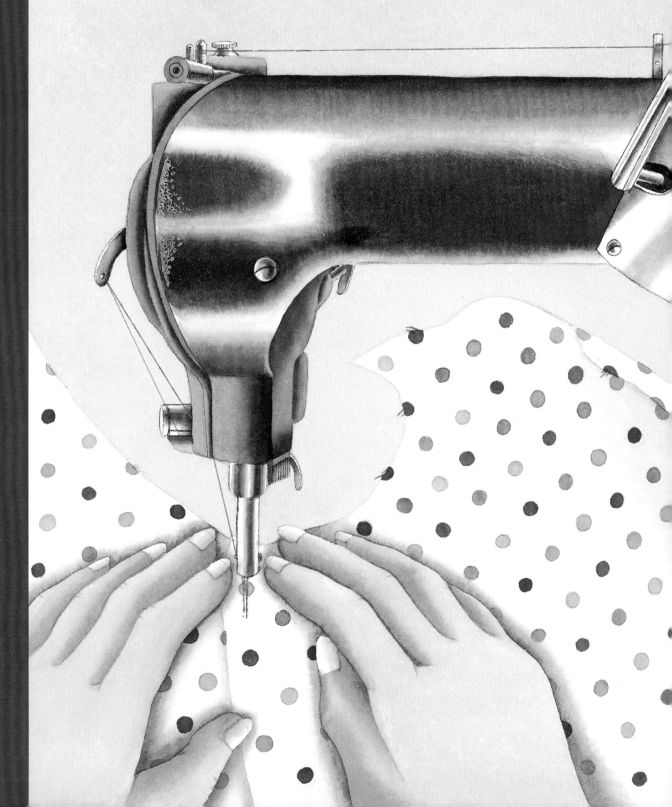

S stands for Sewing machine
and the way most clothes are sewn,
whether you buy them in a store
or stitch them up at home.

Other inventors, like James Gibbs who invented the chain-stitch machine and Augusta Blanchard, inventor of the zigzag stitch, improved the sewing machine. Originally, sewing machines replaced hand stitching in the garment industry. Today related industries use sewing machines and they are in millions of homes worldwide.

Chances are blue jeans are among the clothing items you often wear. You might even have a favorite pair. But do you know jeans have been sewn and sold in America since the 1870s? Around 1850, Levi Strauss left the East Coast for San Francisco along with those hoping to discover gold. He did not want to pan for gold. He wanted to sell household items such as pillows, cloth, and clothing to miners and their families. He became known and respected for his high quality and long-wearing products. Then, in 1872, Jacob Davis, a tailor in Nevada who bought Strauss's fabric, shared a new idea with Strauss: reinforcing work pants with metal rivets. They received a patent for their "Improvement in Pocket Openings" on May 20, 1873—known as the "birthday of blue jeans." Seamstresses sewed those first denim jeans, called "waist overalls," in their homes. Unable to keep up with demand, Levi Strauss opened his first factory in San Francisco—and the rest is history!

T is for Toilet—
a bathroom word we must know
no matter where we are,
in case we have to go!

Most readers use toilets. You might use expressions such as lavatory, restroom, bathroom, loo, water closet, head, or john, and special words for what you do there. The words may vary, but the toilet has been nearly universal since people began living in one place and had running water. With the exception of Queen Elizabeth I, whose godson Sir John Harington invented a flush toilet for her in 1596, most Europeans and settlers in America used outhouses, also known as "privies" before toilets were invented. During the night they relied on chamber pots kept next to their beds. Slaves and servants emptied the chamber pots in the streets and rivers or carried them to cesspools. People were unaware of germs, pollution, and hygiene.

While many people believe that English plumber John Crapper invented the toilet, according to historians, he did not. It took many inventors, patents and improvements to create the modern-day toilet. In 1875, James Henry and William Campbell patented their version in the United States. Toilet paper on rolls, invented by the Scott Paper Company, followed in 1890. On average, today's homes use one roll every five days.

The umbrella did not change the world yet it represents everyday inventions we take for granted but ones that come in handy. Beulah Louise Henry held 49 patents, but she invented more than 100 items, mainly for women and children. As an umbrella inventor, she uniquely added snap-on covers of different colors so women could match their "parasols" with their clothing.

We use umbrellas when it is rainy and often when it is sunny. Have you ever noticed how many colors and patterns of umbrellas you can find on the street?

U
u

What does a beautiful Umbrella do? U
It brings us to the letter U
then shades the sun
and keeps the rain from soaking through.

Explorers in South America returned with bottles filled with latex found in the bark of rubber trees. Nicknamed "gum elastic," this white gooey substance bounced and stretched. It was waterproof. It seemed ideal for making waterproof boots, elastic suspenders, and stretchy rubber bands.

The excitement over this new import craze weakened as the seasons changed. Consumers and manufacturers realized that latex products turned gooey and sticky when temperatures rose. In cold temperatures, products became brittle and breakable.

Charles Goodyear, determined to change rubber into a usable product, devoted his energy to this ambition. Hard financial times did not stop him. He was often penniless and even landed in debtor's prison for not paying his bills. Eventually and by accident, he invented vulcanized rubber during an experiment at the kitchen stove. Steam heat and sulfur changed the sticky goo into the durable product we know today.

Inventor Charles Goodyear
takes us to letter V
for Vulcanizing rubber
from the gooey latex of the rubber tree.

If this one seems tricky—let me explain.
Goodyear experimented until he found
the way to improve rubber
and keep tires round.

He earned the patent for vulcanized rubber in 1844. The word Vulcan comes from ancient times—the Roman god of fire. Goodyear might have become a millionaire in manufacturing, but he chose to stay with his invention, thinking of hundreds of uses for his product that we still use today. People infringed on his patent in the United States and he did not seek foreign patents in time to protect his process overseas. He died in debt, as he was before his invention, but he thought of himself as wealthy in another sense. He knew others would keep his ideas alive. He thought his contributions to society, not money, were the true measure of wealth.

Vv

W

Henry Ford developed the assembly line method of building autos, making cars cheaper to manufacture and purchase, but many other inventors improved cars. They are the ones who added safety, comfort, and ease.

Mary Anderson invented the windshield wiper even before the Model T rolled off Ford's assembly line. In 1903, she invented windshield wipers for trolley conductors so they could clear their windows while driving. By 1916, windshield wipers became standard equipment. Charlotte Bridgewood improved the idea with the first automatic wipers in 1917.

It took more than 50 years for intermittent windshield wipers, ones that swished at slower speeds, to become popular. Robert Kearns patented his invention in 1967, but could not convince automakers to use his idea. Later, car manufacturers violated patent laws by using his invention without permission. Mr. Kearns received millions of dollars from Chrysler and Ford Motor Companies for their use of his unique invention.

Windshield wipers are handy during rain and snow. With seat belts and better tires, cars are safer as they go.

Charles Kettering invented the electric starter in 1917. His invention replaced the difficult hand crank method. By 1929, car radios developed by William Lear made listening to the radio while driving commonplace.

Garrett Morgan, inventor of the gas mask, patented an automatic traffic light to make driving safer in 1923. His light had three signals: Stop, go, and stop in all directions.

Nils Bohlin, a safety engineer for Volvo, became a lifesaver when he invented lap and shoulder harness seatbelts. His invention replaced the less safe single lap belt design. Patented in 1959, his invention saves thousands of lives and prevents even more injuries. Before his death in 1999 he saw his idea spread to all auto manufacturers and lead to mandatory seatbelt laws in most states and countries.

In 1952 John Hetrick obtained a patent for his airbag design after he and his family were in a single car accident. Hetrick had a good idea, but not a great invention. Alan Breed, who invented the airbags we use today, began working on his invention in 1968. He is still working on car safety. Among his latest contributions to automobile safety is the side airbag.

In 1895 William Conrad Roentgen could hardly believe what he discovered: X-rays. Because so little was known about these early radiation waves, Roentgen called them X (standing for the unknown) rays, short for radiation. Combined with photography, the rays passed through some substances such as skin to reveal a picture of what was beneath. This German scientist won the first Nobel Prize in Physics for his invention, but he never patented his X-ray technology. American scientist William D. Coolidge invented the "Coolidge tube." His invention allowed technicians to use the tiny electrical waves safely and conveniently. He received 83 patents for other ideas, too.

Assisted tomography, simply called CAT scan, combines the X-ray with computer technology to make three-dimensional images. These advances help doctors diagnose medical conditions such as cancer.

Today, X-rays go beyond the health field. Airports worldwide use X-rays to search luggage quickly. You might wonder what X-rays are and how they can "see" inside a suitcase. Simply put, X-rays are tiny light waves that are absorbed by dense objects.

X stands for X-ray
used by doctors to diagnose aches and pains.
At airports, X-rays help baggage handlers
check luggage before loading it on planes.

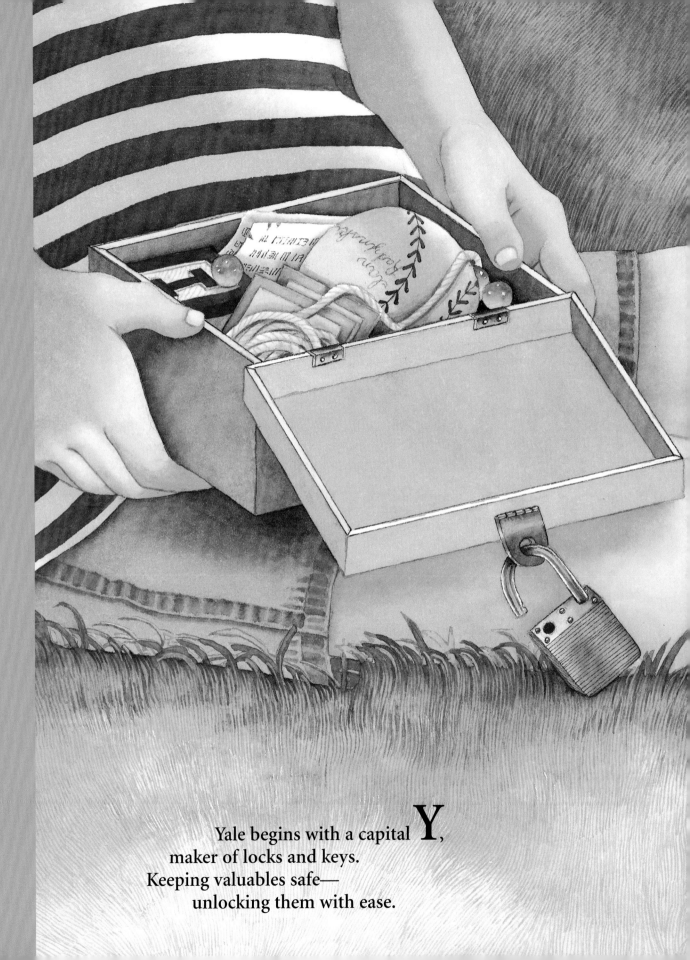

If you use a combination lock on your school locker or to keep your bike safe, you might be using Linus Yale's invention. His ideas came from his inventor father, whose name was also Linus, and a long history of locks dating to 4,000 years ago. Egyptians created huge locks but they were not handy for everyday needs. After the older Linus died, his son continued his work. He invented the cylinder pin-tumble we still use today.

Yale begins with a capital Y,
maker of locks and keys.
Keeping valuables safe—
unlocking them with ease.

We have found inventions for every letter of the alphabet. Some are more important than others. Now we end with zipper, an obvious but not world-changing choice. Or is it? The zipper demonstrates how even simple inventions progress through change and revision. At various times during its history, the zipper held different names. Elias Howe's patent in 1851 described the zipper as "an automatic, continuous clothing closure." Whitcomb Judson invented the "clasp locker" for shoes. He took his invention to the World's Fair in 1893, but it was not a hit.

In 1917 the name became the "separable fastener" when Gideon Sundback patented another version. B.F. Goodrich Co. changed the name to zipper and used them on rubber boots. Several decades later, the clothing industry, especially men's trousers, updated its button styles to ones using zippers. Once it did, the zipper became a household word.

Today, a Japanese family company called YKK manufactures nearly half of all zippers in the world—about 2.7 billion each year!

Zz

It is time to thank the handy Zipper as we end with letter Z.
Think of everything that zips—
jackets, notebooks, and cases for CDs.

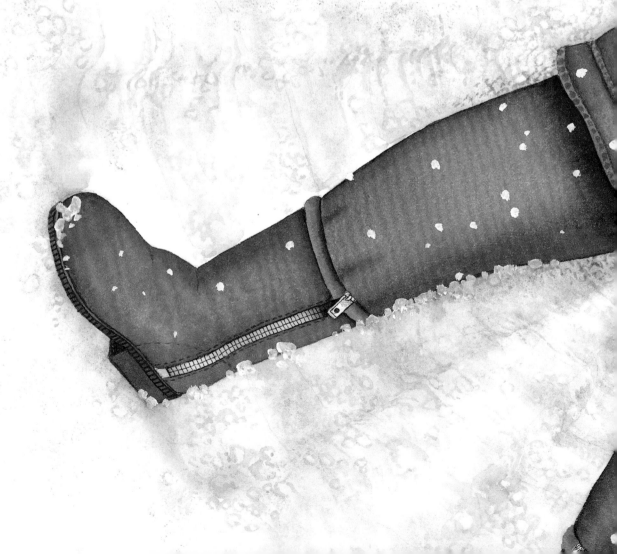

There are more ideas to explore
and inventors waiting to be met,
but you have come to the end
of our invention alphabet.

An Imagination Full of Questions

1. Why do some inventions, such as Kevlar® begin with a capital letter?

2. What invention made blue jeans popular in the United States?

3. What does the height, 1,776 feet, of New York's Freedom Tower represent?

4. What does the expression "the real McCoy" mean?

5. Where is the Inventors Hall of Fame and Museum located?

6. What invention led to the computer modem?

7. What invention is nicknamed "lazy bones?"

8. What are aluminum's unique qualities?

9. Where does the word *vulcanized* come from?

10. Garrett Morgan invented the gas mask. Another of his inventions help drivers. What is it?

11. Why is it important to receive a patent?

12. What is Braille and why was it invented?

13. Dynamite was a powerful invention. Its inventor, Alfred Nobel, sought to recognize others who affected the world with their powerful and positive accomplishments. What was his legacy?

14. Where are some places you can visit, personally or online, to learn more about inventions?

Answers

1. Once registered with the United States Patent and Trademark Office, names of specific brands, designs and inventions become proper nouns. Capitalize them and add the trademark symbol.

2. The copper rivets patented by Levi Strauss and Jacob Davis.

3. It is also the date of the United States' independence.

4. It means "genuine" or of the highest quality, and originated when Elijah McCoy's invention of the railroad lubricating cup was imitated by other manufacturers. Consumers wanted to make sure they were getting the "real McCoy"—not a copy of it.

5. Akron, Ohio

6. The telephone

7. The remote control

8. Aluminum is lightweight, rust-free, recyclable, and inexpensive.

9. It stems from the Roman god of fire, Vulcan.

10. The automatic traffic light

11. Patents protect the inventor by preventing others from making or selling the same idea in the country where the patent is held.

12. Braille is a code made of raised dots, called cells. Louis Braille invented the system so that he could read quickly.

13. He started the Nobel Prizes, including the Nobel Peace Prize.

14. Visit the Smithsonian National Air and Space Museum, Washington, DC (http://www.nasm.si.edu/wrightbrothers), or other Smithsonian Institution museums, such as the Lemelson Center for the Study of Invention and Innovation at the National Museum of American History (www.invention.smithsonian.org). Spend the day at the Inventors Hall of Fame and Museum in Akron, Ohio (http://www.invent.org) and check out http://nobelprize.org/nobel/nobelmuseum to learn more about the Nobel Peace Prize. The museum, where the dynamite molds are on exhibit, is located in Old Town in the center of Stockholm, Sweden.

P is for Patent.
It provides protection—
a way to share the idea
but hold onto the invention.

English courts provided patents for early settlers in America. Sybilla Masters obtained a patent for her method of making cornmeal to preserve the corn given to her by Native Americans. Though her husband received the patent, English courts acknowledged her invention in 1715. The first U.S. patent was granted in 1790.

Since then there have been changes to patent laws, but receiving a patent still protects the inventor. The United States Patent and Trademark Office records a detailed account of the invention "to exclude others from making, using, offering for sale, or selling the invention throughout the United States or importing the invention into the United States" once the inventor makes his idea public. Sometimes inventors obtain patents in other countries, too.

The U.S. Patent and Trademark Office suggests taking these five steps before applying for a patent: Make sure your idea is new and practical, keep records to prove your invention, search both literature and patents of related inventions, and then study these findings. The fifth step is preparing and filing for your patent. Usually an expert helps prepare the application. It takes about two years to hear if the application has been accepted or rejected. If the application is turned down, the inventor can go back to work, changing the invention, the application, or both.

I is for Idea: An Inventions Alphabet touches upon a few of the many interesting, lifesaving, and even quirky inventions that shape and affect our lives. There are millions more—important ones with unique stories behind them. For example, Gertrude Elion knew she wanted to find cures for cancers and other diseases after her grandfather and then her mother died of cancer. Elion invented the method scientists use to create new drugs. Using her own technique, she invented lifesaving drugs including one that puts childhood leukemia in remission. She and her coworker, George Hitchings, won the Nobel Peace Prize for their work in 1988.

Marcia Schonberg

Author Marcia Schonberg inspires creativity and imagination in readers as they learn about inventions in *I is for Idea: An Inventions Alphabet*. While not an inventor herself, Marcia became fascinated with the amazing contributions and dedication of inventors and their work during her many years as a children's writer. After more than a dozen nonfiction titles and hundreds of published freelance articles to her credit, she presents this unique collection, written in similar style to her other award-winning Sleeping Bear Press titles, *Cardinal Numbers: An Ohio Counting Book* and her ever-popular, *B is for Buckeye: An Ohio Alphabet*.

Just as her home state of Ohio became the focal point of many of her previous titles, *I is for Idea* includes researchers honored in the Inventors' Hall of Fame, located within Inventure Place in Akron, Ohio. Able to weave interesting facts and timelines of numerous inventions into her verse and commentary, she connects youngsters to inventors from all over the world and throughout many historical time periods. Marcia lives in both Central Ohio and Naples, Florida.

Kandy Radzinski

Kandy Radzinski received her Masters of Fine Arts from East Texas State University. She taught art at Central Washington State College and the University of Tulsa. Kandy has illustrated children's books, posters, greeting cards, and even a six-foot penguin. Her art has been described as "quirky realism" and can be seen at www.kradzinski.com. She also illustrated *S is for Sooner: An Oklahoma Alphabet*, published in 2003 by Sleeping Bear Press.

She lives in Tulsa, Oklahoma, has two Scottie dogs, Miss Moe and Kirby, a son named Ian, and a husband, Mark. Ian is a third-degree black belt and Kandy is a second-degree black belt in Tae Kwon Do.